BRIDAL BLISS

A Guide to Choosing Your Perfect Wedding Dress

PUBLISHED BY: Success Publication SAR

Alicia Hernandez-Whyle

Copyright © 2024 by Alicia Hernandez-Whyle

All rights reserved.

No part of this publication may be reproduced in any form or by any electronic or mechanical means, including information storage and retrieval systems, without written permission from the author, except for the use of brief quotations in a book review.

BRIDAL BLISS

Alicia Hernandez-Whyle

Table of Contents:

Introduction 5

Setting the Stage for a Stress-Free Experience 8

Understanding Your Body Shape..20

Dressing for Your Body Shape 28

Exploring the Enchantment of Fabrics..42

Seasonal Bridal Dress Selection..49

Timeless Elegance 57

Contemporary Couture: The Trendy Bride 68

Accesorizing with Elegance 78

Reflecting Personal Style...84

Perfecting the Fit..91

Budgeting Brilliance..97

Shopping Etiquette for Bridal Gowns...107

ABOUT AUTHOR..112

Introduction

Congratulations on your engagement! As you begin on this exciting journey towards your wedding day, you'll soon realize that one of the most important decisions you'll make is choosing the perfect wedding dress. "Bridal Bliss: A Guide to Choosing Your Perfect Wedding Dress" is here to be your trusted companion throughout this process.

This book is designed with you in mind, providing invaluable insights, tips, activities, and advice to help you navigate the intricate world of wedding dress shopping with confidence and ease. But before we dive into the depths of bridal fashion, let me share a personal story that inspired the creation of this book.

When I was planning my own wedding, I faced a dilemma that many brides encounter: the quest for an affordable yet beautiful wedding dress. As I pursued my degree at the time, finances were tight, leaving me with limited options. Desperate to find a gown within my budget, I turned to online shopping and purchased a dress from a Chinese supplier on eBay.

The moment the package arrived, my excitement quickly turned to heart-wrenching disappointment. I discovered the poor quality material, the ill-fitting silhouette that did nothing to complement my body, and the glaring lack of attention to detail. It was a devastating realization that the bargain price I paid came at the steep cost of sacrificing quality and craftsmanship. Despite my overwhelming doubts and the sinking feeling in my stomach, I felt trapped, knowing I had no choice but to walk down the aisle in that dress. My dreams shattered.

That experience stayed with me, igniting a passion to ensure that no bride should ever feel disheartened on her wedding day. So, I made it my mission. That same year I got married, I decided to open my own online bridal boutique. My goal was simple: to ensure every bride walked down the aisle in a beautiful gown that made her feel confident, regardless of her budget.

Throughout my years as a bridal consultant and boutique owner, I've had the privilege of working with brides of all shapes, sizes, and backgrounds. With each bride, I learned something new, gaining insights into different body types and the styles that complement them. Through over a decade of experience, I've come to appreciate the transformative power of the right gown and the joy it brings to a bride's special day.

Now, I'm excited to pass on that knowledge to you. "Bridal Bliss" is not just a guide; it's a labor of love, born from my own journey and fueled by a desire to make your wedding dress shopping experience as magical as it should be.

BRIDAL BLISS

Each chapter is crafted to address your concerns, clarify any questions you may have, and instill you with confidence. From understanding your body shape to decoding bridal terminology, the aim is to help you embrace this once-in-a-lifetime experience with joy and excitement.

Whether you're embarking on this journey solo or with your nearest and dearest by your side, "Bridal Bliss" is your go-to resource for creating cherished memories, celebrating your unique beauty, and ultimately finding the dress of your dreams. Let this book be your guiding light as you step into bridal boutiques, browse through bridal magazines, and envision yourself walking down the aisle in the gown that captures your heart.

Embrace the magic of this special time in your life, and let "Bridal Bliss" guide you as you go on this exhilarating adventure of choosing the perfect wedding dress.

Alicia Hernandez-Whyle

Chapter One

Setting the Stage for a Stress-Free Experience

In the pursuit of the perfect wedding dress, setting the stage for a stress-free and joyful experience is essential. This chapter delves into the importance of creating an environment filled with excitement and joy as you start your search for your dream dress.

As you set off in search of the dress that perfectly fits your unique style and personality, get ready to be amazed by the endless possibilities in bridal couture. Stepping into the world of bridal couture is like entering a realm of dreams, where every gown holds the promise of turning your vision into reality.

Imagine yourself surrounded by a dazzling array of gowns, each more exquisite than the last. From flowing silhouettes adorned with intricate lace to sleek designs embellished with shimmering details, the options are boundless.

With each gown you slip into, feel the excitement grow with every delicate stitch and graceful curve. Each fitting becomes a celebration of your journey toward that magical moment when you'll walk down the aisle in your perfect dress. As you try on each gown, imagine yourself walking towards your beloved, surrounded by the beauty and joy of your wedding day.

Navigating the Emotional Rollercoaster

The process of finding your wedding dress can stir up a whirlwind of emotions, from excitement to anxiety. But by staying calm and embracing joy, each step becomes smoother and more fulfilling. Take a moment to breathe deeply, soaking in the happiness of the experience.

Wedding dress shopping is not just about finding the perfect gown; it's a beautiful opportunity to connect with your loved ones and create memories that will last a lifetime. Share laughs, hugs, and smiles with your closest friends and family, making every moment count.

Above all, a stress-free and joyful atmosphere empowers you to make decisions that truly reflect your inner self. With each choice, you're one step closer to discovering the dress of your dreams, filled with emotions that resonate deeply.

As you begin the dress shopping journey, laugh with your friends, revel in the excitement of each fitting, and treasure the memories you're creating together. These moments are precious gems that you'll hold dear forever.

Yet, amidst this sea of beauty, there are moments of struggle, moments where the dream of finding the perfect dress feels like an impossible task. One such moment unfolded with Sonya, a bride I had the privilege of working with as a bridal consultant.

Sonya's Story: Finding Your Voice

Sonya entered the boutique with excitement, surrounded by a crowd of supporters. Her mom imagined her as a fairytale princess in a classic ball gown, while her mother-in-law favored slimming sheath dresses, and Sonya leaned towards modern designs. The clash of opinions left Sonya feeling lost among conflicting visions.

Trying on dress after dress, Sonya grew more frustrated. She felt torn between her preferences and those of her entourage, struggling to make her own decision. Feeling disappointed and unsure, Sonya left the boutique without a dress. However, after a few weeks, she returned alone, determined to find clarity.

When Sonya came back, she seemed more determined. Once she was alone, free from outside pressures, Sonya was able to focus and find clarity in her choices.

Finally, it happened. Sonya stood before the mirror, radiant and resplendent in her chosen gown. In that moment, I saw the joy flood back into her eyes, replacing the doubt and uncertainty.

Sonya's journey emphasizes the importance of a stress-free approach to dress shopping.

While having your loved ones with you can be wonderful, it's crucial to consider their personalities and whether their opinions will help or hinder your decision-making process. Sometimes, going solo can allow you to truly connect with your own desires and preferences. Trust your instincts, and don't be afraid to take some time alone to find your own voice amidst the sea of voices around you.

Guiding Tips for a Joyful Experience

Start Early

Start your dress shopping early to have enough time for exploring and pondering. This way, you can avoid feeling rushed and have time for multiple fittings and alterations to ensure your gown fits perfectly.

Research Styles

Research different dress styles before going to the boutique. Knowing what you like will make choosing easier and more enjoyable.

Setting a Realistic Budget

One of the cornerstones of a stress-free dress shopping experience is establishing a budget and sticking to it. By determining your financial boundaries, you narrow down your choices, ensuring that every gown you try on aligns with your financial plan.

Limiting Entourage Size

Limit the number of people you bring with you to those whose opinions you really value. Too many opinions can be confusing and stressful. Stick to your trusted confidants who can support you.

Handle Conflicting Opinions Gracefully

Conflicting opinions during wedding dress shopping are common, especially from family and friends with differing views on the perfect dress. Stay calm and listen, even if you disagree. Showing respect for different opinions creates a positive atmosphere.

Choosing the Right Boutique

Choose a bridal boutique with a good reputation and a wide range of styles. Knowledgeable staff can transform the shopping experience and guide you through the process with expertise and enthusiasm.

Wearing Comfortable Attire

Wear comfortable clothes and shoes. Opt for easy-to-slip-on shoes and lightweight clothing. Being comfortable will make trying on dresses easier and more enjoyable.

Staying Open-Minded

While it's essential to have preferences, remain open to trying on dresses suggested by the consultant. You may find yourself pleasantly surprised by something outside your initial vision.

Scheduling Appointments

Plan ahead and schedule appointments to secure personalized attention from consultants. This will help create a calm atmosphere focused on you.

Celebrating Small Wins

Throughout the process, celebrate every victory, no matter how small. Finding things you like about a dress, even if it's not the perfect one, makes the journey more positive and exciting, showing you the way forward.

Taking Breaks

Take breaks if you feel overwhelmed. This will help you stay calm and refreshed for the rest of the day.

Having Realistic Expectations

Understand that the perfect dress may not reveal itself immediately. Embrace patience and trust in the process, knowing that with each dress tried on, you're one step closer to discovering the gown of your dreams.

Using these tips will take you on a journey filled with laughter, love, and anticipation.

To streamline the wedding dress shopping process and ensure you find the gown of your dreams, let's outline a detailed timeline to guide you through each step.

Wedding Dress Shopping Timeline

12–9 Months Before the Wedding

Research and Inspiration Phase

Spend time exploring various sources of inspiration, such as bridal magazines, wedding websites, and social media platforms like Pinterest and Instagram.

Consider your personal style, body type, and wedding theme when gathering dress ideas.

Take note of specific details you like in dresses, such as neckline styles, skirt shapes, and fabric choices.

Use online tools like virtual dress try-on apps or dress design software to experiment with different styles.

Initial Boutique Visits

Research local bridal boutiques and read reviews to find reputable establishments.

Call ahead to schedule appointments, especially if you're planning to visit on weekends or during peak seasons.

Invite trusted friends or family members to accompany you to provide feedback and support during your dress shopping experience.

8–7 Months Before the Wedding

Narrowing Down Choices

Reflect on your initial dress shopping experiences and identify the styles, fabrics, and details you gravitate towards.

Consult your wedding budget and prioritize the features that are most important to you in a dress.

Request to revisit your favorite dresses at the bridal boutiques for a second or third try-on session.

Take detailed notes and photos of each dress you try on to aid in your decision-making process.

Finalizing the Dress

Once you've found a dress that resonates with you, carefully examine its construction, quality, and comfort.

Discuss any desired modifications or customizations with the bridal consultant, such as altering the neckline, adding sleeves, or changing the color.

Clarify the pricing, payment schedule, and delivery timeline for the dress, including any additional fees for alterations.

Begin exploring options for bridal accessories that will complement your chosen dress, such as veils, headpieces, jewelry, and shoes.

6–5 Months Before the Wedding

First Fitting and Alterations

Schedule your first fitting appointment with a skilled seamstress or the alterations department at the bridal boutique.

Bring along the specific undergarments and shoes you plan to wear with the dress to ensure proper fitting.

Communicate openly with the seamstress about your preferences and any concerns you may have regarding the fit or style of the dress.

Discuss the scope of alterations needed, such as taking in or letting out seams, adjusting hem lengths, and adding or removing embellishments.

Accessorizing

Use your dress fitting appointments as an opportunity to experiment with different accessory combinations, such as veils, headpieces, belts, and jewelry.

Consider the overall aesthetic of your wedding and choose accessories that complement the style and theme.

Take into account factors like hairstyle, makeup, and venue when selecting accessories to ensure cohesiveness with your bridal look.

Purchase or order your chosen accessories.

4–3 Months Before the Wedding

Second Fitting and Finalizing Details

Attend your second fitting appointment to assess the progress of the alterations and make any necessary adjustments.

Evaluate the fit and comfort of the dress, paying close attention to areas that may require further tweaking.

Provide feedback to the seamstress regarding any desired changes or alterations to ensure the dress meets your expectations.

Confirm the timeline for completing alterations and schedule any additional fittings or appointments as needed.

Final Touches

Confirm the availability of your chosen accessories and ensure they align with the finalized alterations to your dress.

Coordinate hair and makeup trials to finalize your bridal look and ensure that your accessories complement your overall appearance.

Arrange for any necessary steaming, pressing, or cleaning of your dress to ensure it looks pristine on your wedding day.

2 Months Before the Wedding

Final Fitting and Pickup

Attend your final fitting appointment to verify that all alterations have been completed satisfactorily and that the dress fits perfectly.

Confirm the pickup or delivery arrangements for your dress and accessories, taking into account any travel logistics or storage considerations.

Ensure that you have a designated space to store your dress safely until the wedding day, protecting it from wrinkles, stains, and damage.

1 Month Before the Wedding

Final Preparations

Conduct a final try-on session with your dress to ensure that everything is in order and that you feel comfortable and confident in your bridal ensemble.

Double-check your accessories, undergarments, and shoes to ensure that everything is accounted for and ready for the wedding day.

Communicate with your wedding planner, coordinator, or venue staff to finalize the logistics of transporting and dressing in your wedding attire on the big day.

On the Wedding Day

Getting Ready

Begin your wedding day preparations early to allow ample time for getting dressed and completing any last-minute touches.

BRIDAL BLISS

Enlist the help of your bridal party or trusted individuals to assist you in getting into your dress and accessorizing.

Take a moment to savor the excitement and anticipation as you admire yourself in the mirror, knowing that you've found the perfect dress for your special day.

In summary, the wedding dress shopping timeline provides a structured approach to finding the perfect gown for your special day. From initial research to final fittings, each step ensures a smooth and enjoyable experience.

By following this timeline, you'll be well-prepared to make confident decisions and create a bridal look that reflects your unique style and personality.

Having laid the groundwork for a stress-free bridal journey, our focus now shifts to understanding your body shape.

Chapter Two

Understanding Your Body Shape

In the process of bridal gown shopping, it's empowering for a bride to recognize her unique body shape. Every curve and contour is a canvas waiting to be adorned with a gown that enhances your natural features. Here, you will learn to understand your body shape and select styles that will make you radiate confidence on your special day. Embracing your body shape isn't just about finding the perfect dress; it's about celebrating your individuality and feeling comfortable and beautiful in your own skin.

This chapter is designed to empower brides with the knowledge and confidence to celebrate their unique body shapes when shopping for their wedding dress. By providing personalized insights and tips for different body shapes, it fosters self-assurance in brides as they explore wedding dress options.

Confidence and grace will emanate from a wedding dress that truly complements a bride's unique silhouette. Every bride should embrace her body shape with pride and confidence; this will allow her to find a wedding dress that makes her feel like the most beautiful version of herself on her wedding day.

Let's explore the various body shapes and discover the ideal wedding dress silhouettes for each.

Hourglass

The hourglass body shape is characterized by a well-defined waist, balanced proportions between the bust and hips, and a curvy silhouette.

For an hourglass body shape, ideal dress styles include mermaid or trumpet silhouettes to accentuate curves.

When dressing an hourglass body shape, consider highlighting the waist with a fitted bodice and steering clear of excessively voluminous skirts that might conceal curves.

Pear Shape

The body features narrower shoulders and busts, wider hips and thighs, and a less defined waistline.

Wedding dress styles for this body type include A-line or ball gown silhouettes to balance proportions and empire waistlines to draw attention upward.

To enhance the silhouette for this body type, consider highlighting the upper body with embellishments or details and selecting fabrics that skim over the hips without adding bulk.

Apple Shape

The body exhibits a fuller bust and midsection, along with slimmer hips and legs and a less defined waistline.

For this body type, ideal dress styles include empire waistlines to create definition, V-neck or sweetheart necklines to elongate the torso, and A-line or princess-cut silhouettes to balance proportions.

Opt for dresses featuring vertical details to elongate the body, while avoiding fabrics that cling too tightly around the midsection. Seek out styles that divert attention from the midsection, such as those adorned with embellishments on the neckline or skirt.

Rectangle Shape

A rectangle body shape is characterized by balanced proportions with minimal waist definition, a straight, athletic-build silhouette, and similar measurements for the bust, waist, and hips.

For a rectangle body shape, A-line or ball gown silhouettes help create the appearance of curves. Dresses with details at the waist can create the illusion of curves. Additionally, dresses with draped fabric, ruching, ruffles, lace, or embellishments add dimension and enhance the figure.

Choose dresses with texture or volume to add dimension. Details such as ruffles, lace, or embellishments can add volume to the bust or hips, creating the illusion of curves. Look for dresses with detailing such as ruffles, sashes, belts, or pleats to add interest and shape. Avoid overly boxy or shapeless styles that can accentuate a straight silhouette.

Inverted Triangle Shape

The inverted triangle body shape is characterized by broad shoulders and busts, a narrow waist and hips, and a defined waistline.

Ideal dress styles for an inverted triangle body shape include A-line or ball gown silhouettes to balance proportions, off-the-shoulder or V-necklines to soften the shoulders, and dresses with full or gathered skirts to add volume to the lower body.

For this unique silhouettes brides should choose dresses that highligh the waist with embellishments or a defined waistline to create curves, choose skirts that add volume to the lower body, and avoid overly voluminous or puffy sleeves, as they can emphasize broad shoulders.

Now that we've explored various body shapes and their ideal dress styles, let's now delve into the Body Shape Quiz, which was prepared to help you identify your unique silhouette.

Body Shape Quiz: Discover Your Unique Silhouette

Instructions: Answer the following questions to the best of your ability. Be honest and accurate in your responses to determine your body shape.

Bust Measurement:

A. 34 inches or less

B. 35-37 inches

C. 38-40 inches

D. 41 inches or more

Waist Measurement (at the smallest part):

A. 24 inches or less

B. 25-27 inches

C. 28-30 inches

D. 31 inches or more

Hip Measurement (at the fullest part):

A. 34 inches or less

B. 35-37 inches

C. 38-40 inches

D. 41 inches or more

Shoulder Width:

A. Narrower than hips

B. Equal to hips

C. Slightly wider than hips

D. Much wider than hips

Proportions:

A. Balanced proportions, defined waist

B. Narrower shoulders, wider hips

C. Broader shoulders, narrower hips

D. Straighter, less defined waistline

Body Contours:

A. Curvy, defined waistline

B. Fuller hips, thighs wider than shoulders

C. Broader shoulders, less defined waistline

D. Straighter, minimal curves

Preferred Dress Fit:

A. Fitted styles that highlight curves

B. A-line or ball gown styles that balance proportions

C. Empire waist or styles that define the waistline

D. Styles that create the illusion of curves or add volume

Dominant Feature:

A. Curvy bust and hips, defined waist

B. Fuller hips, narrower shoulders

C. Broad shoulders, less defined waist

D. Balanced measurements, straighter silhouette

Scoring:

For each A answer, give yourself 1 point.

For each B answer, give yourself 2 points.

For each C answer, give yourself 3 points.

For each D answer, give yourself 4 points.

Results:

8-15 points: You have an Hourglass body shape.

16-22 points: You have a Pear body shape.

23-29 points: You have an Apple body shape.

30-32 points: You have a Rectangle body shape.

33-40 points: You have an Inverted Triangle body shape.

After completing the quiz, you can tally your points and determine your body shape based on the scoring guide provided.

Your body shape is unique and deserves to be celebrated as you search for the perfect wedding dress. By understanding and embracing your silhouette, you'll be able to select outfits that flatter your figure and express your personal style.

Armed with the knowledge from this chapter, go forth with pride and confidence, knowing that your wedding dress will not only flatter your figure but also reflect the beauty of your individuality.

With a thorough understanding of your body shape for achieving flawless bridal elegance, we now transition to the chapter on dressing specifically to complement your unique physique.

Chapter Three

Dressing for Your Body Shape

Selecting the right wedding dress silhouette is crucial, as it significantly contributes to enhancing your overall bridal appearance. Every body shape is unique, and choosing a silhouette that complements yours can accentuate your best features and flatter your silhouette.

Understanding your body type and choosing the appropriate wedding dress silhouette can highlight your curves, create proportion, and ultimately make you feel stunning as you walk down the aisle.

Camile's Story

BRIDAL BLISS

As a bridal consultant at my boutique, I had the privilege of working with numerous brides, each with their own unique story. To elaborate on the importance of finding the right silhouette, let me share one of my past brides stories with you. As a plus-size bride with measurements of 30W bust, 26W hips, and 24W waist, Camile faced some great challenges on her journey to finding her dream dress.

Camile's disappointment with other salons stemmed from the limited options available to plus-size brides like her, the few dresses designed for her body shape in her size, and the judgmental staff's rude facial expressions. Numerous salons either lacked dresses in her size or offered limited selections that didn't align with her vision.

As Camile stepped into my boutique, tears brimmed in her eyes. I had spotted her from afar, sitting in her car, her shoulders shaking with sobs. Camile's entire demeanor seemed drained, envoking a sense of hopelessness. She appeared apprehensive, uncertain if this would be another disappointing ordeal.

As I approached Camile, I sensed her desperation. "You'll leave here with a gorgeous gown," I assured her, my voice soft but firm, willing her to believe it. Upon meeting her, I swiftly recognized her body type and instinctively understood the ideal silhouette for her. With empathy and understanding, I guided her towards the A-line silhouette.

Though her exact size wasn't in stock (the largest size being 26W), I improvised. Assisting her into the 26W gown, I knew it wouldn't fit perfectly without corseting or zipping up, but I wanted to offer her a glimpse of how the A-line silhouette would look on her. This silhouette suited Camile's body type perfectly. As she stood before the mirror, I pointed out how the dress hugged her bust and waist before gracefully flowing outward, creating a romantic and feminine silhouette that highlighted her best features.

After settling on the silhouette, I delve into the finer details. I inquired about Camile's preferences regarding sleeves, beading, and other embellishments. It was her dress, her special moment, and I wanted to ensure every detail was aligned with her vision.

Engaging her in the process, I could see her excitement intensify with each decision. It was a collaborative effort, a shared journey towards finding the perfect wedding dress. Although she didn't leave with her dress that day, Camile left with the assurance that her dress would exceed all her expectations.

We coordinated with the designer to customize the gown to her measurements and preferences, ensuring a perfect fit. In the weeks that followed, I collaborated tirelessly with the designer to craft a gown tailored to Camile's unique measurements. When she returned for her fitting, the transformation was breathtaking. The joy and excitement radiating from her as she twirled in her gown echoed throughout the boutique.

Drawing inspiration from Camile's journey, brides embarking on their dress search should keep in mind the importance of understanding their body type and exploring silhouettes that highlight their best features. Whether you're a plus-size bride like Camile or have a different body type, remember that there's a silhouette out there that will make you feel stunning. Try on different styles, and don't be afraid to step out of your comfort zone.

Also, keep in mind that if one salon cannot help you, don't hesitate to try another. Trust your instincts and select the dress that resonates with your inner and outer beauty.

Just as Camile found the right silhouette for her body type, let's help you find yours.

Ball Gown:

Ideal for brides seeking a timeless and regal look, the ball gown silhouette features a fitted bodice and voluminous skirt that accentuate the waist while camouflaging the lower body. It creates a balanced silhouette by highlighting the waist and adding volume to the skirt, making it perfect for brides with hourglass or pear shapes.

A-line:

The A-line silhouette is a versatile and universally flattering style for wedding gowns. With a fitted bodice that gently flares out from the waist, it creates a natural and flattering shape that skims over the hips and thighs. Offering structure and definition to the waist, it provides a classic and timeless look suitable for various body types.

Mermaid:

The fitted bodice and flared skirt of a mermaid silhouette hug the curves and accentuate the natural waistline, creating a stunning hourglass shape, making it perfect for hourglass and petite brides.

Sheath:

Sleek and form-fitting, the sheath gown follows the natural contours of the body, creating a streamlined and elongated look. Ideal for slender or athletic brides, it offers a modern and effortless aesthetic, highlighting natural curves with sophistication.

Fit and Flare:

Combining the elegance of a mermaid gown with the ease of movement of an A-line skirt, the fit and flare silhouette accentuates the waist and hips. Flattering for hourglass figures and petite frames, it offers a balance of glamour and comfort.

Empire:

Featuring a high waistline just below the bust, the empire silhouette creates a lengthening effect on the body. Skimming over the midsection and hips, it flatters apple-shaped figures or those with petite frames. Recommended for pregnant brides, it offers a high waistline for comfort and a flattering look.

Now that we've discussed how to dress for your body shape, let's now explore enhancing your bridal look with the right neckline.

Enhancing Your Bridal Look with the Right Neckline

Choosing the perfect wedding dress is an exhilarating experience, and selecting the right neckline plays a crucial role in enhancing your overall bridal look. Necklines not only frame your face but also have a significant impact on the appearance of your body shape. Understanding which neckline complements your body type can make all the difference in achieving a stunning and flattering bridal ensemble.

Just as our bodies boast individual contours and curves, so too do our neckline choices, which play a crucial role in accentuating our features and enhancing our bridal look.

Let's journey into the art of selecting the perfect neckline to complement various body shapes.

Sweetheart Neckline:

This charming and timeless style suits hourglass and pear-shaped figures. The heart-shaped dip at the bust beautifully defines curves while balancing proportions. It draws attention to the décolletage area, highlighting the well-defined bust and waist, and is perfect for hourglass and pear shapes.

V-neckline:

The V-neckline elongates the neck, creating a flattering vertical line that's perfect for inverted triangle and rectangle-shaped bodies. This neckline helps balance broad shoulders and adds length to the upper body, creating a more proportionate silhouette. It also adds interest to the torso of rectangle-shaped figures, creating the illusion of curves.

Off-the-Shoulder Neckline:

For pear and hourglass-shaped bodies, the off-the-shoulder neckline is a stunning choice. By exposing the shoulders while framing the neckline elegantly, it highlights the collarbones and shoulders while drawing attention away from the hips and thighs.

This adds a touch of romance to the overall look, accentuating curves for hourglass figures and balancing proportions for pear shapes.

Scoop Neckline:

The soft and rounded scoop neckline flatters most body types but is particularly suitable for apple-shaped figures. By drawing attention away from the midsection and towards the face and neckline, it helps create a balanced and proportionate appearance.

Halter Neckline:

The halter neckline, featuring straps that wrap around the neck, creates a chic and sophisticated look, adding curves and interest to the upper body. This makes it perfect for athletic or rectangle-shaped bodies that may lack definition in the bust area.

Boat Neckline:

The wide and horizontal boat neckline sits at or near the collarbone, balancing broad shoulders and creating the illusion of curves at the waist. It draws attention upwards towards the face and neckline, making it an ideal choice for apple and rectangle shapes.

Now that we have concluded our discussion of necklines, let's continue our journey into the world of sleeves, another essential element that adds personality and elegance to your bridal ensemble.

Bridal Sleeve Selection

Sleeves serve a dual purpose, not only enhancing a bride's appearance but also ensuring her comfort and confidence. They bring grace and practicality to bridal attire, making them indispensable for brides of all body types.

Join us as we explore how sleeves can beautifully complement every bride, ensuring both style and comfort as she walks down the aisle.

Cap Sleeves:

Cap sleeves are short, covering only the top of the shoulder. They are ideal for petite brides or those with narrow shoulders, creating the illusion of broader shoulders and balancing out the silhouette.

Short Sleeves:

Extending slightly past the shoulder, typically ending above the elbow, short sleeves are suitable for most body types. They provide coverage while allowing freedom of movement, perfect for brides seeking arm coverage without feeling too confined.

Three-Quarter Sleeves:

Extending to about mid-forearm, three-quarter sleeves offer more coverage than short sleeves but less than full-length sleeves. Flattering for brides with fuller arms or those seeking a modest option, they allow the arms to be showcased while still providing coverage.

Long Sleeves:

Extending to the wrist, long sleeves offer maximum arm coverage. They are perfect for brides desiring full coverage or those with slender arms looking to add dimension to their silhouette. Long sleeves can also balance out wider shoulders.

Off-the-Shoulder Sleeves:

Situated below the shoulders, often with a draped or ruffled effect, off-the-shoulder sleeves are ideal for brides with narrow shoulders. They showcase collarbones and shoulders while also balancing out broader hips by drawing attention upwards.

Illusion Sleeves:

Made of sheer fabric, often adorned with lace or embellishments, illusion sleeves create the appearance of bare skin while providing coverage. Suitable for various body types, they offer a delicate and romantic look, particularly flattering for brides seeking the illusion of bare arms with subtle coverage.

Puff Sleeves:

Characterized by volume at the shoulder and tapering down to a fitted cuff at the wrist, puff sleeves are perfect for brides looking to add volume to their shoulders or balance out wider hips. They create a feminine and whimsical look, suitable for both petite and curvy brides.

In conclusion, our journey through the realm of bridal gown elements has been enlightening. We began by discussing the significance of understanding unique body shapes and finding the right silhouette to enhance each bride's natural beauty. Next, we explored a selection of neckline styles, each tailored to different body shapes, and delved into sleeve options designed to flatter various figures.

Armed with this insight, brides can approach their dress hunt with assurance, equipped to fashion a bridal look that exudes individuality and sophistication. By embracing their body shape and preferences, they can pinpoint the perfect silhouette, neckline, and sleeves to curate a wedding dress that captures their essence and personal style.

To help you better understand your wedding dress preferences, let's dive into an activity designed to help you identify the features you would love in your wedding dress.

BRIDAL BLISS

Preference Ranking Exercise:

This activity is designed to clarify your preferences and guide your dress selection process.

Instructions:

Rank each dress feature based on your preferences, with 1 being the highest priority and 5 being the lowest priority. Consider what aspects are most important to you when searching for your dream dress.

Neckline Styles

A. Sweetheart

B. V-neck

C. Off-the-shoulder

D. High neck

E. Strapless

Rank:

1.1 _____

1.2 _____

1.3 _____

1.4 _____

1.5 _____

Sleeve Length

A. Sleeveless

B. Cap sleeves

C. Short sleeves

D. 3/4 sleeves

E. Long sleeves

Rank:

2.1 _____

2.2 _____

2.3 _____

2.4 _____

2.5 _____

BRIDAL BLISS

Skirt Types

A. A-line

B. Ball gown

C. Mermaid/trumpet

D. Sheath

E. Tea-length

Rank:

3.1 _____

3.2 _____

3.3 _____

3.4 _____

3.5 _____

Fabric Types

A. Lace

B. Satin

C. Tulle

D. Chiffon

E. Organza

Rank:

4.1 _____

4.2 _____

4.3 _____

4.4 _____

4.5 _____

Embellishments

A. Beading

B. Floral appliqués

C. Embroidery

D. Sequins

E. None; I prefer a minimalist look

Rank:

5.1 _____

5.2 _____

5.3 _____

5.4 _____

5.5 _____

After ranking each dress feature, review your preferences to gain clarity on what aspects are most important to you when searching for your dream wedding dress.

Use this exercise as a guide to prioritize your preferences and communicate them effectively with bridal consultants or designers. Adjust the features and options as needed to match your specific preferences and style.

Chapter Four

Exploring the Enchantment of Fabrics

In the enchanting world of wedding dress fabrics, each choice weaves a unique tale, capturing dreams, desires, and the promise of everlasting love.

Join us as we explore the realms of fabric, unveiling the emotional and practical allure of each fabric to guide you toward finding the perfect ensemble for your fairytale day.

Kisha's Dream: Tulle and the Quest for the Perfect Dress

Among the brides I helped was Kisha, a plus-size bride who had a clear vision and adored tulle fabric; her excitement and anticipation were evident. With eyes alight, she presented a photo of her dream dress: a grand ball gown made of tulle.

Even though I knew that this style might not be the most conventionally flattering choice for her size 20 frame, I remained silent, respecting her unwavering determination to bring her fairytale vision to life.

Despite Kisha's excitement, the tulle ball gown didn't live up to her expectations. The dress overwhelmed her, making her appear larger than she was. She longed for the 'wow' effect but found herself feeling self-conscious.

We moved on to A-line dresses, hoping for a better fit, but even the A-line tulle versions she insisted on failed to meet her expectations. With each gown, her frustration became increasingly visible.

Realizing the need for a change, I gently suggested trying a different fabric. Despite Kisha's initial reluctance, she agreed to experiment with satin.

As she slipped into the luxurious satin ball gown, her expression transformed. The dress flattered her figure beautifully, enhancing her natural curves without adding bulk.

In that moment, I witnessed the transformative power of fabric. As she admired her reflection in the mirror, I knew we had found the perfect gown to fulfill her dreams of elegance and grace on her special day.

But I didn't forget Kisha's initial love for tulle. To incorporate her beloved fabric, we added delicate tulle sleeves and a neckline, infusing her gown with the ethereal quality she had always envisioned. It was a perfect blend of her dream fabric with the one that truly complemented her figure, creating a gown as unique and beautiful as she was.

Kisha's journey shows how important it is to pick the right fabric and style for a wedding dress. She learned that the type of fabric can really change how a dress looks and feels. At first, she liked tulle, but later found out that satin suited her better. This taught her the value of trying different options until she found what worked best for her. Kisha's story reminds us to embrace our uniqueness and choose a dress that matches our body shape and personal taste.

Transitioning from the narrative about Kisha's journey, we can seamlessly shift our focus to discussing the significance of different fabric choices in choosing the perfect wedding dress.

Silk: Elegance and Sophistication

Silk, often seen as a symbol of luxury, elegance, and refinement, is a favorite among brides for its luxurious feel and timeless charm. Known for its smooth texture and lustrous sheen appearance, silk drapes the body with understated elegance, offering a range of styles from sleek to flowing. Whether you see yourself in a slim-fitting gown that follows your curves or a romantic ball gown with cascading layers, silk adds a touch of sophistication to every bridal look.

Moreover, its natural shimmer catches the light beautifully, making every moment captured in photos look stunning. Silk works particularly well for brides with hourglass or pear-shaped figures, accentuating curves while providing a flattering silhouette.

Choosing a silk wedding dress not only ensures a stunning appearance but also respects long-held bridal customs.

Lace: Romance and Femininity

Lace, known for its detailed patterns and delicate designs, has always been linked with romance and femininity. Whether adorning the bodice, neckline, sleeves, or hemline, lace brings a touch of graceful elegance to any wedding outfit. Its soft, lightweight texture drapes gracefully over the body, offering comfort and freedom of movement. From classic Chantilly lace to vintage-inspired Alençon lace, each style carries a hint of nostalgia and tradition, connecting to wedding customs of the past.

Apart from its pretty look, lace often holds sentimental value, becoming a treasured family keepsake passed down through generations.

Tulle: Whimsy and Playfulness

Tulle, often seen as the fabric of dreams, brings a sense of whimsy, lightness, and playfulness with its delicate netting and airy texture. Known for its soft, flowing quality, tulle adds a magical touch to any wedding outfit, creating an atmosphere of ethereal romance and enchantment. Whether cascading in layers from a voluminous ball gown or floating gently in a sleek A-line silhouette, tulle captures the imagination with its dreamy allure.

Its versatility shines in various styles, from classic ball gowns to modern fit-and-flare designs, allowing brides to express their unique style and personality. Additionally, tulle's gentle texture and lightweight feel ensure comfort and freedom of movement.

Depending on where it's placed within a wedding dress, tulle can enhance different body types, particularly for brides with petite frames or those aiming to add volume to their silhouette.

Satin: Understated Glamour

Satin, known for its timeless elegance and luxurious feel, exudes understated glamour in every detail. With its smooth texture and subtle sheen, satin adds sophistication to any bridal ensemble, creating a sense of effortless allure. Whether draped in a sleek silhouette or embellished with intricate details, satin captivates with its refined elegance.

Satin complements various body types since its versatility allows for a range of styles, from classic ball gowns to modern mermaid silhouettes, ensuring every bride finds her perfect match. Moreover, satin's ability to catch the light enhances the overall aesthetic of wedding photos, ensuring every moment is captured with radiant beauty.

Beyond its visual appeal, satin holds symbolic significance, symbolizing purity, grace, and elegance.

Crepe: Modern Elegance and Timeless Sophistication

Crepe, known for its simple elegance and flexibility, offers a unique matte finish and gentle texture that bring a modern touch to bridal ensembles. Light but sturdy, crepe creates sleek silhouettes that accentuate the bride's figure with clean lines and understated grace.

Whether you choose a sleek straight gown or a well-fitted bridal jumpsuit, crepe offers versatility with different styles and designs, allowing for plenty of personalization.

This fabric is particularly flattering for brides with an hourglass or pear-shaped body, as it accentuates curves while providing a smooth silhouette.

Moreover, crepe's comfort and resilience ensure a flawless appearance from ceremony to reception, allowing brides to move with confidence and poise.

Organza: Ethereal Beauty and Delicate Elegance

Organza, with its crisp feel and light, transparent quality, creates a romantic and dreamy atmosphere. Its transparent layers add depth and flow to bridal ensembles, giving a feeling of light beauty and delicate elegance.

Whether used as an overlay for a ball gown skirt or a delicate sleeve detail, organza lends a graceful and sophisticated aura to every wedding dress. Its versatility allows for various styles, from soft and flowing to structured and sleek, ensuring that every bride finds her perfect look.

Organza fabric is particularly flattering for brides with a slender or athletic body type, as it adds volume and creates a soft, feminine silhouette.

Moreover, organza's light-catching qualities enhance the beauty of wedding photos, ensuring that every moment is filled with radiant splendor.

Chiffon: Airy Grace and Effortless Charm

Chiffon is a fantastic choice for brides aiming for a soft, romantic vibe on their big day. Its light and breezy feel creates a graceful silhouette that works for any wedding style, be it classic or modern.

Whether you're going for a simple look or something more intricate with ruching, ruffles, or pleats, chiffon can bring that extra touch of elegance to your bridal ensemble.

Chiffon is perfect for outdoor or beach weddings, adding to the dreamy atmosphere with its ability to catch the light and flow gently in the breeze.

For brides with slender or athletic figures, chiffon works wonders by adding a soft, ethereal quality to their look. It enhances their natural beauty, giving off that fairy tale-like aura as they walk down the aisle.

As we finish discussing bridal fabrics, it's important to always consider your individual body shape and size, and to seek guidance from bridal consultants—they're here to assist you in finding the perfect wedding dress.

Whether it's silk, lace, tulle, satin, crepe, organza, chiffon, or a mix, let your gown reflect your unique style and personality. After all, it's about finding the wedding dress that makes you feel truly beautiful, inside and out.

Having explored the enchantment of various fabrics, we now turn our attention to the art of selecting bridal dresses that perfectly align with each season.

Chapter Five

Seasonal Bridal Dress Selection

Selecting the ideal wedding dress means considering the season and venue, essential factors that influence the overall mood and setting of your special day. Each season and venue offers its own unique charm when it comes to choosing the right attire.

Let's go deeper into the enchanting interplay between seasonal considerations and wedding venues, guiding you towards finding the perfect wedding dress that harmonizes with your chosen setting.

When choosing the appropriate attire for the season, brides should always consider the following:

Comfort: No bride wants to be shivering in a strapless gown in the middle of winter or sweating profusely under layers of tulle in a scorching summer heatwave. Choosing the appropriate attire for the season ensures comfort throughout the day.

Feasibility: Venues can vary from grand ballrooms to rustic barns, each with its own ambiance and requirements. The dress should complement the venue, both aesthetically and practically. For instance, walking through a sandy beach in a heavy ball gown might not be the most practical choice.

Visual Appeal: Visual Appeal: Every season has its own colors, textures, and ambiance. The dress should harmonize with the surroundings, enhancing the overall atmosphere and theme of the wedding. For example, a winter wedding might call for a gown made of rich satin or velvet, adorned with intricate beadwork that reflects the season's elegance, while a summer wedding would be complemented by a light, airy chiffon dress that captures the breezy, bright nature of the season.

Now that we understand the importance of considering the season and venue, let's dive into the specifics, starting with the enchanting splendor of spring weddings.

Spring Splendor

Spring weddings symbolize renewal and blooming flowers, embodying the essence of new beginnings and fresh starts. Spring weddings are often held in gardens, vineyards, or botanical settings. Choose a dress that complements the natural beauty of your surroundings. Dress the part with these tips:

Fabrics and Silhouettes: Opt for light and airy fabrics like chiffon, organza, or lace, with A-line, mermaid, or ball gown silhouettes. Embrace floral motifs or intricate lace details.

Neckline and Sleeves: Embrace the whimsy of spring with sweetheart necklines, off-the-shoulder styles, or delicate lace sleeves.

Colors: Ivory, blush pink, soft lavender, or mint green are perfect for spring weddings.

Summer Serenity

Summer weddings exude sunshine, warmth, and endless possibilities. Whether it's a beach resort, a rooftop garden, or a countryside estate, choose a dress that suits the vibe of the venue. Beat the heat in style with these suggestions:

Fabrics and silhouette: Choose breathable fabrics such as organza, chiffon, and tulle that offer both elegance and comfort amidst the summer heat. Consider flowy silhouettes such as a-line, sheath, or mermaid silhouettes for easy movement and a flattering fit.

Neckline and Sleeves: Keep cool with strapless or spaghetti strap styles, or embrace the bohemian vibe with flutter sleeves or a halter neckline.

Colors: For summer weddings, brides often opt for wedding dresses in pure white, ivory, champagne, or blush pink, reflecting the warmth and romance of the season.

Autumn Ambiance

Autumn weddings set a cozy and romantic backdrop with golden leaves and crisp air. It is often held in rustic barns, vineyards, or historic estates. Embrace the season's warmth and charm with these tips:

Fabrics and silhouette: Luxurious fabrics like velvet, satin, or crepe are perfect for autumn. Consider ball gowns, sheath or trumpet silhouettes adorned with intricate lace overlays.

Neckline and Sleeves: Stay cozy with long sleeves, illusion necklines, or high necklines that offer both warmth and elegance.

Colors: Popular wedding dress colors for this season include ivory, champagne, taupe, and rich shades of gold and bronze.

Winter Enchantment

Winter weddings evoke a sense of magic and romance, with twinkling lights and snow-covered landscapes. This season, weddings are usually held in cozy cabins or grand ballrooms, each offering its own unique ambiance. Dress for the season in style with these recommendations:

Fabrics and Silhouette: For winter weddings, opt for luxurious fabrics like silk satin, velvet, or faux fur for a glamorous and warm ensemble. Choose ball gown or sheath silhouettes with intricate beadwork, embroidery, or layers of tulle for a mesmerizing look.

Neckline and Sleeves: Stay warm and chic with long sleeves, high necklines, luxurious fur accents, or elegant wraps and capes.

Colors: Embrace the classic elegance of winter with classic ivory, cozy champagne, romantic blush, bold burgundy, or sophisticated navy blue.

In conclusion, whether your wedding is surrounded by blossoms or bathed in frost, your choice of dress should reflect the season and venue, creating a timeless and romantic ensemble.

Now that we've explored the intricacies of seasonal bridal dress selection, let's put your knowledge to the test with a quiz.

BRIDAL BLISS

This quiz will assess your understanding of the key concepts discussed in Chapter Five, focusing on how different seasons and venues influence the choice of bridal attire.

Remember, the goal is not just to test your memory but to reinforce your understanding of how seasonal considerations play a vital role in creating the perfect bridal ensemble.

So, without further ado, let's dive into the quiz and see how well you've grasped the principles of seasonal bridal dress selection!

Multiple-Choice Questions

What are the three main considerations emphasized in the chapter for selecting the appropriate bridal attire?

A. Fabric, Style, Price

B. Comfort, Feasibility, Visual Appeal

C. Color, Length, Designer

D. Size, Shape, Brand

Which of the following venues is not typically associated with spring weddings?

A. Gardens

B. Vineyards

C. Beach Resorts

D. Botanical Settings

What type of silhouette is recommended for summer weddings to ensure easy movement and a flattering fit?

A. Ball Gown

B. Mermaid

C. A-Line

D. Trumpet

Which fabric is suggested for autumn weddings to capture the season's warmth and charm?

A. Chiffon

B. Velvet

C. Organza

D. Tulle

What colors are popular for winter weddings, according to the chapter?

A. Pastel Shades

B. Neon Colors

C. Jewel Tones

D. Earthy Tones

II. True or False Questions:

True or False: Spring weddings symbolize renewal and blooming flowers.

BRIDAL BLISS

A. True

B. False

True or False: For summer weddings, brides often opt for heavy fabrics like velvet or satin.

A. True

B. False

True or False: Long sleeves and high necklines are recommended for summer weddings to keep cool.

A. True

B. False

True or False: Autumn weddings are often held in beach resorts.

A. True

B. False

True or False: Winter weddings evoke a sense of magic and romance with snow-covered landscapes.

A. True

B. False

III. Matching Questions:

Match the venue with the appropriate season:

A. Rustic Barns 1. Winter

B. Beach Resorts 2. Spring

C. Grand Ballrooms 3. Summer

D. Cozy Cabins 4. Autumn

Options:

A. 1, B. 3, C. 2, D. 4

A. 4, B. 1, C. 3, D. 2

A. 3, B. 4, C. 1, D. 2

A. 2, B. 3, C. 1, D. 4

With our discussion on Seasonal Bridal Dress Selection behind us, we can now turn our attention to the enduring charm of timeless elegance.

Chapter Six

Timeless Elegance

Finding the right balance between timeless elegance and trendy designs is key to choosing the perfect wedding dress. This means considering your personal style, the lasting beauty of classic features, and the wish to capture the essence of the current moment.

Timeless elegance embodies styles and elements that have transcended generations, maintaining their allure and relevance over time.

Now, we'll delve deeper into the individual components that give a gown its timeless appeal.

Classic Silhouettes

Ball Gown: The ball gown silhouette has captivated brides for centuries with its voluminous skirts and fitted bodices. Today, the ball gown remains as popular as ever, transcending generations and trends to maintain its status as a bridal classic.

Its association with romance, elegance, and fairy tale dreams ensures its enduring allure for modern brides. Whether walking down the aisle of a grand cathedral or exchanging vows in a rustic barn, brides continue to choose the ball gown for its ability to turn their wedding day into a timeless celebration of love and enchantment.

A-line: Emerging in the 1950s, the A-line silhouette, characterized by its fitted bodice and gently flared skirt, has become a bridal classic. Its universally flattering shape complements various body types, making it a popular choice for brides seeking a timeless and elegant look.

Sheath: The sheath silhouette, also known as the column or straight silhouette, originated in the early 20th century. This silhouette's ability to flatter the figure while offering versatility and comfort is what makes it timeless.

Minimalist Design

Minimalist wedding dresses embody simplicity, clean lines, and understated elegance. These dresses feature sleek, uncomplicated silhouettes, allowing the bride's natural beauty to shine. Whether through straight, geometric shapes or gentle curves that accentuate the bride's figure, clean lines create a modern and sophisticated aesthetic.

Minimalist dresses possess a lasting quality, ensuring they won't look dated and making them a popular choice for brides seeking enduring sophistication.

Versatile enough for various wedding styles, they can be easily accessorized to reflect the bride's individual preferences.

Lace and satin

Lace and satin together create a beautiful blend of textures and emotions, elevating wedding dresses beyond mere clothing. Lace, with its delicate patterns and vintage charm, evokes timeless romance, reminiscent of old love stories. From the softness of Chantilly lace to the intricate details of Guipure lace, each type adds elegance.

Satin, known for its smooth, shiny texture, introduces a touch of luxury and sophistication. Whether used as the main fabric or for subtle accents, satin enhances the dress's appeal, making it look refined.

These materials possess an ageless allure that transcends trends and exudes sophistication. They can be styled into various silhouettes, from simple sheaths to fuller ball gowns, catering to individual tastes.

Ultimately, combining lace and satin in wedding dresses captures the essence of romance and elegance, making them popular choices for brides seeking a timeless and beautiful look for their big day.

Iconic Necklines

Iconic necklines exude an undying charm, embodying timeless elegance that captivates brides worldwide. Whether it's the classic V-neck, the graceful off-the-shoulder style, or the enchanting sweetheart cut, these necklines are meticulously selected by brides for their ability to enhance their natural beauty with a touch of sophistication.

They serve as a bridge between tradition and modernity, offering a timeless appeal that transcends fleeting trends. Brides gravitate towards these necklines not only for their aesthetic appeal but also for their flattering fit, ensuring that every bride feels radiant and confident on her big day.

With their enduring allure and classic charm, these necklines remain eternal favorites, promising to enchant brides for generations to come.

Vintage Inspiration

Vintage inspiration in wedding dresses brings the charm of past eras into the modern day. Brides can choose styles from different decades, each with its own unique flair. From the flapper dresses of the 1920s with their beaded embellishments to the tea-length dresses of the 1950s that exude a sweet, retro vibe, vintage styles offer a variety of looks.

The bohemian dresses of the 1970s, with their flowing fabrics and relaxed fit, appeal to brides seeking a more laid-back feel. Vintage wedding dresses not only provide timeless elegance but also allow brides to make a statement by embracing the beauty and uniqueness of bygone times.

Traditional Details

Traditional details are key to creating a timeless sense of elegance in wedding dresses. These elements, passed down through generations, add depth and richness, giving the gown a sense of heritage and sophistication. Delicate lace patterns, intricate beadwork, and subtle shimmering pearls are just a few examples that transform wedding dresses into works of art. Each stitch tells a story filled with cultural significance and sentimental value. Features like buttons down the back, a long train, or a cathedral-length veil bring a classic beauty that never goes out of style.

Finding a dress with the right traditional details is like discovering a piece of family history. It creates a gown that not only fits the bride but also carries the essence of her roots, making her wedding day a timeless celebration of love, joy, and cherished traditions.

To show the importance of traditional details in timeless elegance, let's meet Emily, another bride I had the pleasure of working with.

Alicia Hernandez-Whyle

Emily's Story

Emily's childhood was a tapestry of cherished moments spent flipping through old wedding albums with her grandmother. The timeless elegance of the classic wedding dresses captured her imagination, particularly her grandmother's A-line gown with delicate lace sleeves and a sweetheart neckline.

When her grandmother passed away, Emily felt a profound sense of loss. As her own wedding day approached, she yearned to honor her grandmother's memory in a meaningful way.

Deciding to incorporate a piece of her grandmother's wedding dress into her own gown, Emily, with her mother's blessing, carefully removed a portion of the preserved lace.

Upon the recommendation of a previous bride, Emily stepped into my boutique, her heart set on finding a gown that would allow her to integrate the cherished lace.

Excitedly, she shared her idea with me, expressing how incorporating her grandmother's lace would make her feel like she was carrying a piece of her beloved grandmother with her down the aisle.

After trying on numerous gowns, Emily finally found "the one." It was a beautiful sleeveless A-line dress with a sweetheart neckline. The decision to customize the dress with her grandmother's lace was met with excitement, and we eagerly set to work on creating the finished masterpiece.

Carefully, we added sleeves made from her grandmother's lace, seamlessly blending them into the dress. To further accentuate the sweetheart neckline, we fashioned a choker neckpiece from the lace, completing the look. When Emily returned for her fitting, her reaction surpassed our expectations.

After the wedding, Emily returned to my boutique, eager to share her photos and express her gratitude. Her joy was palpable as she reflected on the significance of her gown. To her, it was more than just a dress; it was a connection to the past, present, and future. She expressed hope that one day her own granddaughter might draw inspiration from her wedding photos.

As she left, I felt a sense of fulfillment, knowing that I had played a part in creating a timeless memory for Emily and her family.

Her decision to choose a timeless design and incorporate her grandmother's lace honored her family's history and created a lasting memory. Her gown was not only a tribute to past grace but also a celebration of love passed down through generations.

In conclusion, timeless elegance in wedding fashion remains an enduring choice for brides seeking a classic yet sophisticated look on their special day. From iconic necklines to classic silhouettes, these timeless elements continue to stand the test of time.

With their ability to flatter a range of figures and evoke a sense of timeless beauty, these timeless elements will undoubtedly remain beloved by brides for generations to come.

Now that we've explored the essence of timeless elegance in bridal fashion, let's dive into a practical exercise to help you determine your preference for classic wedding dress styles.

Alicia Hernandez-Whyle

Classic Wedding Dress Style Preference Checklist

By going through this checklist, brides can identify their preferences and priorities, helping them narrow down their options and find the perfect wedding dress that reflects their individuality and vision for their special day.

Silhouette

1. [] Ball gown: voluminous skirt with a fitted bodice.
2. [] A-line: fitted bodice with a gently flared skirt resembling the shape of the letter "A."
3. [] Sheath: sleek and figure-hugging silhouette with minimal flare.

Neckline

1. [] Sweetheart: heart-shaped neckline accentuating the décolletage.
2. [] V-neck: v-shaped neckline elongating the neck and torso.
3. [] Scoop: classic rounded neckline offering warmth and comfort.
4. [] Boat neck: wide and shallow curve across the collarbones for a vintage-inspired look.

5. [] Off-the-shoulder: romantic neckline exposing the shoulders while framing the face beautifully.

Fabric

1. [] Lace: delicate and intricate fabric adding a sense of timeless romance.

2. [] Satin: smooth and luxurious fabric for a touch of elegance and sophistication.

3. [] Tulle: lightweight and airy fabric perfect for creating volume and ethereal charm.

4. [] Chiffon: flowy and soft fabric ideal for a relaxed and effortless look.

5. [] Organza: crisp and lightweight fabric with a subtle sheen for a modern touch.

Details

1. [] Minimalist: clean lines and understated elegance with subtle embellishments.

2. [] Intricate beading: elaborate beadwork adding shimmer and texture to the gown.

3. [] Floral appliqués: romantic and feminine embellishments inspired by nature.

4. [] Embroidery: handcrafted designs adding depth and intricacy to the fabric.

5. [] Dramatic train: statement-making train for added grandeur and elegance.

Color

1. [] Traditional white: classic and timeless hue symbolizing purity and innocence.

2. [] Ivory: soft and warm shade with a vintage-inspired feel.

3. [] Champagne: subtle and sophisticated color with a hint of warmth.

4. [] Blush: romantic and feminine hue adding a touch of softness and warmth.

5. [] Something blue: incorporate a subtle blue accent for a unique and meaningful touch.

Style Inspiration

1. [] Vintage glamour: inspired by the elegance and charm of past eras.

2. [] Bohemian chic: relaxed and free-spirited style with a modern twist.

3. [] Classic romance: timeless and sophisticated look with a focus on tradition.

4. [] Modern elegance: sleek and minimalist aesthetic for a contemporary feel.

5. [] Fairytale princess: dreamy and enchanting style inspired by fairytales and romance.

Personal Preferences

1. [] Comfort: prioritize comfort and ease of movement for a stress-free wedding day.

2. [] Venue: consider the wedding venue and setting when choosing the dress style and details.

3. [] Body type: highlight your best features and flatter your figure with the right silhouette.

4. [] Budget: set a budget and stick to it while exploring different dress options.

5. [] Sentimental value: incorporate meaningful details or traditions into the dress design for a personal touch.

Alicia Hernandez-Whyle

Chapter Seven

Contemporary Couture: The Trendy Bride

In this chapter, we explore the exciting world of modern wedding dresses, where tradition meets new ideas and classic beauty mixes with bold, new styles. We look at the latest trends in bridal fashion, featuring daring cuts, new fabrics, and unique designs that push the boundaries of what a wedding dress can be.

This chapter will help you decide if you lean more towards timeless elegance or modern flair.

Imagine the confident stride of a bride in a sleek, fitted mermaid dress, or the ethereal beauty of a gown adorned with delicate lace and detailed beading.

These trends are more than just about fashion; they're about expressing yourself and feeling empowered.

Let's delve into the features of contemporary bridal wear that have brides buzzing with excitement.

Bold Silhouettes

Modern brides are gravitating towards bold silhouettes in wedding dresses to express their unique personalities and styles. These dramatic shapes offer a personalized and distinctive look, allowing brides to stand out and showcase their individuality. Let's discuss it more in depth.

Mermaid: The mermaid silhouette takes center stage, reflecting contemporary elegance and self-assured style. Its sleek, curve-hugging design appeals to brides seeking a bold yet sophisticated look. This silhouette embodies the modern bride's desire for individuality, offering a canvas for personal expression through simple details or intricate embellishments.

Huge Ball Gown: In modern bridal fashion, the ball gown silhouette reigns supreme, epitomizing drama and extravagance. With its voluminous skirts and fitted bodices, this silhouette commands attention, offering brides a captivating and show-stopping presence. The cascading trains of a ball gown exude drama and sophistication, making it the ultimate choice for brides who seek to make a bold and unforgettable statement on their wedding day.

Fit and flare: Modern brides choose fit and flare dresses for their flattering silhouette, comfort, and versatility. These dresses allow for easy movement and come in various designs, from minimalist to embellished, catering to different styles. With their blend of elegance and contemporary flair, fit and flare dresses perfectly embody the modern bride's desire for both sophistication and practicality on her wedding day.

When considering bold silhouettes, you must budget wisely, considering the potential higher costs of bold silhouettes, and seek professional guidance from a bridal stylist for expert advice and a perfect fit.

Unique Necklines

In recent years, wedding dresses with unique necklines have become very popular. This change is driven by brides' desire to express their personal style and stand out on their special day. Let's look at some necklines modern brides are leaning toward.

Asymmetric Necklines: These necklines feature one-shoulder or diagonal designs, offering a modern flair to wedding dresses and creating visual interest and uniqueness. Great for broad shoulders or an inverted triangle shape, creating balance.

Illusion Necklines: Illusion necklines utilize sheer fabric with intricate details, creating a delicate and ethereal look. They often feature lace, embroidery, or beading, giving the illusion of skin without revealing too much, making them a popular choice for brides with smaller busts.

High Necklines: High necklines offer a vintage-inspired yet contemporary aesthetic, often incorporating lace or beading for added elegance. They provide coverage while elongating the neck and drawing attention to facial features.

Plunging Necklines: Plunging necklines feature deep V-cuts, adding drama and sensuality to wedding dresses. They accentuate the neckline and décolletage, creating a bold and glamorous statement.

Square or Scoop Necklines: Square necklines feature clean, angular lines, while scoop necklines offer a softer, rounded shape. This neckline is flattering for various body shapes, especially for those with a larger bust.

When choosing a unique neckline for your wedding dress, consider your body shape and comfort first. Moreover, think about how the neckline influences your overall look and accessories, such as jewelry, hairstyle, and veil, to ensure everything works together harmoniously.

Innovative Fabrics:

Modern brides are increasingly drawn to innovative fabrics that blend traditional elegance with modern sensibilities. Let's delve deeper into these types of fabrics.

3D Floral Appliqué: 3D floral appliqué fabric is a popular choice among modern brides seeking a romantic and ethereal look for their wedding day. 3D floral appliqués add depth and dimension to bridal gowns, creating a whimsical and romantic aesthetic.

Metallic Jacquard: Metallic jacquard fabric features intricate woven patterns with metallic threads and is often used in modern wedding dresses to create stunning statement designs.

Stretch Crepe: Stretch crepe is a lightweight, stretchy fabric known for its fluid drape and figure-hugging properties. It's a popular choice for modern bridal gowns due to its versatility and comfort, while allowing for ease of movement.

Sheer Mesh: Sheer mesh fabric adds an element of intrigue and sensuality to bridal gowns with its translucent and lightweight properties. It's often used in illusion details, such as sleeves, necklines, or backs, to create a delicate and ethereal look, making it a popular choice for modern brides seeking a romantic and contemporary style.

Sustainable Fabrics: With an increasing focus on eco-consciousness, modern brides may opt for sustainable fabrics such as organic cotton, hemp, or bamboo silk for their wedding attire.

Silk Mikado: With its luxurious sheen and structured drape, silk Mikado is a modern choice for brides looking for sophistication and elegance.

Velvet: Velvet adds a luxurious and modern touch to bridal gowns, offering both texture and elegance for contemporary brides.

Tulle with Appliqué: Combining the softness of tulle with intricate appliqué designs creates a modern and romantic bridal look.

Neoprene: Known for its sleek and structured look, neoprene provides a contemporary and modern aesthetic to bridal attire.

Laser-Cut Fabrics: These intricate designs create patterns and textures with precision, adding a touch of modern elegance to bridal gowns.

When choosing innovative fabrics for their wedding dress, brides should consider their personal style, comfort, and budget.

Consulting with bridal designers specializing in these fabrics can provide valuable guidance.

Statement Sleeves

Statement sleeves are a captivating trend in modern bridal fashion, offering a touch of drama and unique style to wedding dresses. From voluminous bishop sleeves to intricate lace designs, these sleeves elevate the overall bridal look, allowing brides to express their individuality with elegance and flair.

Let's take an in-depth look at these popular sleeves for modern brides.

Voluminous Puff Sleeves: Modern brides choose voluminous puff sleeves to make a bold statement, adding drama and volume to their gown. These sleeves create the illusion of fuller arms and shoulders, making them especially flattering for slender or petite frames.

Romantic Bishop Sleeves: Characterized by their soft and elegant silhouette, romantic bishop sleeves are favored by modern brides for their timeless yet trendy appeal. They are particularly flattering for those with narrow shoulders or a smaller bust, adding volume and creating a balanced look.

Sleek Trumpet Sleeves: This type of sleeve embodies modern elegance and sophistication, making it perfect for brides who value simplicity and refinement. They accentuate the natural curves of the arms without adding bulk, making them ideal for petite or athletic body types.

Off-the-Shoulder Sleeves: Trendy brides love off-the-shoulder or cold-shoulder sleeves for their allure and sophistication. These sleeves highlight the shoulders and collarbone, offering a flattering and elegant look for various body types.

Flutter or Cap Sleeves: They are favored by brides for their ability to soften the shoulder line and create a gentle silhouette. They add a delicate touch to the gown, complementing a smaller or petite frame.

Detachable Sleeves: Brides appreciate the flexibility of detachable sleeves, whch allow for customization to fit their preferences. These sleeves can be easily attached or removed, offering versatility and adaptability to create different looks.

Unique Details

Modern brides are seeking unique details to make their wedding day truly unforgettable. Let's explore some of these unique details and how they reflect the individuality and style of today's brides.

Distinctive Artistic Details: Brides today are carefully choosing gowns that radiate modern sophistication. Distinctive artisanal details are taking center stage, adding a touch of craftsmanship and individuality to wedding attire. Handcrafted embroidery, customized lace appliqués, and hand-painted designs are just a few examples of the intricate details brides are embracing.

These bespoke elements not only elevate the aesthetic of the dress but also reflect the bride's personal style and vision, making each gown a true work of art.

Luxury and Craftsmanship: One exquisite detail that ensnares the discerning eye of modern brides is unexpected textures that whisper luxury and bespoke craftsmanship. Imagine a gown embellished with intricate beading, lavish 3D floral appliqués, or subtle metallic accents that glisten like rare jewels. These meticulously crafted details imbue the gown with an air of refinement and haute couture savoir-faire, setting it apart as a true work of art in bridal fashion.

Dramatic Back Designs: Most brides of today crave unexpected back designs that evoke a sense of drama and allure, worthy of the most prestigious runways. She seeks out those sublime surprises, such as daring cutouts, exquisite lace-up corsetry, or ethereal illusion panels that enrapture with their couture sophistication.

These captivating elements ensure that the gown commands attention from every angle, leaving an indelible impression as the bride makes her grand entrance and exits in resplendent style.

Non- Traditional Colours

In the changing world of bridal fashion, brides are choosing colors beyond the usual white or ivory. Modern brides are embracing a variety of hues to add uniqueness to their wedding ensemble.

Now that we've introduced the concept of non-traditional colors for wedding dresses, let's delve into the specific hues that are capturing the hearts of modern brides.

Romantic Blush Tones: Blush tones have gained popularity among modern brides for their romantic and ethereal appeal. Soft and feminine, blush hues add a subtle hint of color to the bridal gown, imbuing it with a delicate and romantic charm.

Sophisticated Champagne Hues: Champagne tones exude a sense of luxury and sophistication, evoking the effervescence of celebratory champagne bubbles. These warm, golden hues complement a variety of skin tones and lend an air of understated elegance to the bridal ensemble.

Unconventional Colors: For brides seeking to make a bolder statement, opting for non-traditional colors like deep burgundy, rich emerald green, or even dramatic black can add a striking and unconventional touch to their wedding look. These bold hues command attention and exude confidence, making a memorable impression on guests and setting the stage for a truly unforgettable celebration.

Whether embracing subtle blush tones, sophisticated champagne hues, or daringly bold colors, modern brides are redefining traditional bridal norms and embracing non-traditional colors as a chic and contemporary choice for their special day.

As we conclude our exploration of contemporary bridal couture, it becomes evident that today's brides are presented with a multitude of options that seamlessly blend tradition with innovation. With each element offering a unique expression of creativity and sophistication, you can confidently go through the journey of finding the perfect wedding dress.

Moving from discussions of contemporary style, let's now delve into the art of accessorizing with elegance, where even the smallest details can make a significant impact on the overall bridal ensemble.

Chapter Eight

Accesorizing with Elegance

Introducing the perfect accessories to complement your bridal ensemble is an art form that requires careful consideration to achieve a harmonious and elegant look.

Join us as we explore the intricacies of accessorizing with elegance, ensuring that every accessory enhances the allure of your chosen dress in the right way.

Dress Style and Neckline: When selecting accessories, it's crucial to harmonize them with the style and neckline of your dress. For instance, if your dress features intricate lace or embellishments, opt for subtle accessories like dainty earrings or a delicate bracelet to avoid overshadowing the dress details.

Conversely, if your dress has a minimalist design, you can add interest with more elaborate accessories, such as statement earrings or a bold necklace.

Example: A bride wearing a strapless ball gown with intricate beading may opt for understated stud earrings and a simple bracelet to complement the dress without detracting from its intricate detailing.

Metal Matching: Matching the metal of your accessories with the undertones of your dress is essential for achieving a cohesive look. Warm-toned dresses, such as ivory or champagne, pair beautifully with gold accessories, while cool-toned dresses, like white or silver, complement silver or platinum accessories.

Example: A bride wearing a blush-colored gown may choose accessories in soft, complementary tones, such as rose gold or pale pink, to enhance the romantic allure of her dress.

Balance and Proportion: Maintaining balance and proportion between your dress and accessories is key to creating a visually pleasing aesthetic. If your dress is voluminous or has intricate detailing, opt for more delicate accessories to avoid overwhelming the look.

Similarly, a sleek design can handle larger or statement pieces without appearing cluttered.

Example: A bride wearing a form-fitting sheath dress may opt for a bold statement necklace to add drama and visual interest to her ensemble, balancing the sleek silhouette of her gown.

Consider Your Hairstyle: Your hairstyle can influence the choice of accessories, particularly earrings and headpieces. If you're wearing your hair up, statement earrings can complement the hairstyle and draw attention to your face. For brides with long, flowing hair, subtle accessories like a delicate headpiece or small earrings may be more suitable to avoid competing with the hair.

Example: A bride with an elegant updo may choose chandelier earrings to add sparkle and glamour to her overall look, while a bride with loose curls may opt for a delicate floral hairpin to complement her romantic hairstyle.

Veil Selection: If you're incorporating a veil into your bridal ensemble, it's essential to choose one that complements rather than competes with your dress. Consider factors such as the length, style, and detailing of the veil in relation to the gown to ensure a cohesive and harmonious look.

Example: A bride wearing a sleek and modern gown may opt for a simple fingertip-length veil with minimal embellishments to maintain the clean lines of her dress, while a bride wearing a romantic lace gown may choose a cathedral-length veil with delicate lace trim to complement the dress's romantic aesthetic.

Personal Style and Customization: Let your personal style shine through in your accessory choices, reflecting your unique taste and personality. Customizing jewelry with initials, dates, or meaningful symbols can add a special touch to your bridal ensemble.

Whether you prefer a classic, timeless look or embrace a modern vibe, select accessories that resonate with your individual style and make you feel confident and beautiful on your special day.

Example: A bride with a bohemian-inspired style may opt for nature-inspired accessories such as floral hair vines or leaf-shaped earrings, adding a touch of whimsy and organic charm to her bridal ensemble.

Comfort Matters: Comfort is paramount when selecting accessories, especially considering that you'll be wearing them throughout your wedding day. Choose accessories that are comfortable to wear and won't cause discomfort or distraction during the ceremony or celebration.

Example: A bride may opt for lightweight and hypoallergenic earrings, allowing her to focus on enjoying the special moments of her wedding day without any discomfort or irritation.

Texture and Material Harmony: Think about how different textures and materials can complement or contrast with your dress.

Example: A gown with soft chiffon layers might be beautifully complemented by a pearl necklace or earrings, echoing the fabric's delicate texture. Conversely, a structured satin dress could be paired with sleek, metallic accessories for a modern touch.

Cultural and Symbolic Significance: Incorporate accessories that hold cultural or symbolic meaning.

Example: A bride may wear a piece of jewelry passed down through generations, adding sentimental value to her ensemble. Exploring such meaningful accessories can add depth and significance to the bridal look.

Seasonal and Venue Considerations: Take into account the season and venue of your wedding when selecting accessories.

Example: For a summer garden wedding, light and airy accessories like floral hairpins or delicate anklets may be fitting, while a winter wedding calls for elegant fur wraps or sparkling crystal accents to complement the cozy atmosphere.

Mixing and Matching: Don't be afraid to mix and match different accessories to create a unique and personalized look. Consider layering necklaces or stacking bracelets for added dimension and visual interest.

Mixing metals can also create a modern and eclectic vibe, adding an unexpected twist to your bridal ensemble.

Practicality and Functionality: While aesthetics are important, practicality should also be considered when choosing accessories.

Example: If you'll be dancing the night away, opting for comfortable shoes without sacrificing style is crucial. Selecting a clutch or purse that can hold your essentials without being cumbersome allows you to move freely and enjoy your celebration without worry.

Hair and Makeup Coordination: Collaborate with your hairstylist and makeup artist during accessory selection to ensure that your entire bridal look is cohesive. Consider how your accessories will complement your hairstyle and makeup palette, whether it's adding a touch of sparkle to a sleek updo or choosing statement earrings that enhance your eye makeup.

In conclusion, accessorizing with elegance involves careful consideration of dress style, metal matching, personal style, and comfort. By harmonizing these elements, you can create a cohesive and stunning bridal ensemble that reflects your individuality and enhances your beauty.

BRIDAL BLISS

Trust your instincts, embrace your unique style, and let your accessories elevate your look. Conducting a trial run of your entire ensemble before the wedding ensures everything looks cohesive.

Additionally, coordinating accessories with the groom's attire and the overall wedding theme can further enhance your wedding look.

Moving from accessories, let's now dive into the realm of personal style in bridal fashion, where brides express their individuality.

Chapter Nine

Reflecting Personal Style

Your wedding day is a celebration of love and individuality, and what better way to showcase your uniqueness than through your choice of attire? Your wedding gown is more than just fabric and lace; it's a reflection of your personal style, your journey, and your dreams.

In this chapter, we'll explore how you can infuse your bridal look with your distinctive personality, making your gown truly one-of-a-kind. Whether you prefer classic elegance, modern chic, or something entirely unconventional, we'll guide you through the process of selecting and customizing a gown that tells your story and makes you feel your absolute best on your special day.

Understanding Your Personal Style

The first step in finding a gown that reflects your personal style is to understand what that style is. Whether you are drawn to vintage glamour, modern minimalism, bohemian chic, or classic elegance, your gown should speak to who you are.

Do you gravitate towards classic silhouettes, or are you drawn to more unconventional designs? Take some time to reflect on your everyday wardrobe, your favorite fashion icons, and the pieces you feel most confident wearing. This will provide valuable insights into the elements you might want to incorporate into your wedding gown.

Join us as we explore the subtle distinctions of adding personal touches to your bridal gown, ensuring it embodies your individuality.

Exploring Unique Details

Once you have a sense of your personal style, it's time to think about the details that will make your gown uniquely yours. Incorporating personal touches can transform a beautiful gown into one that tells your story. Consider elements that have sentimental value or cultural significance. Consider incorporating elements that hold special meaning to you and your partner, such as embroidered initials, family heirlooms sewn into the lining, or a patch of fabric from your grandmother's wedding dress.

Even small details, like embroidery of your wedding date or initials, can add a meaningful layer to your gown. This could be as intricate as incorporating your partner's favorite color into the embroidery or as subtle as using a fabric that reminds you of a special place.

These symbolic touches will add depth and personal significance to your dress.

Customization and Bespoke Design

For brides seeking a truly bespoke gown, customization is key. Work closely with a skilled designer or seamstress who can bring your vision to life, from sketching out initial ideas to selecting fabrics, embellishments, and finishing touches. Don't be afraid to think outside the box and explore unconventional design elements that speak to your personality.

Whether it's a dramatic neckline, an unexpected color palette, or whimsical embroidery, your gown should be a reflection of your individuality and creativity.

While customization allows for personal expression, it's essential to strike a balance between trendy elements and timeless features.

Balancing Trends and Timelessness

While it can be tempting to follow the latest bridal trends, it's important to choose elements that you will still love years from now. Balance trendy details with timeless features to ensure your gown remains a cherished part of your memories.

Classic silhouettes and fabrics can be paired with contemporary accents to create a harmonious blend of past and present. While vintage lace can be paired with a modern silhouette, a classic ball gown can feature unexpected details like asymmetrical draping or bold color accents. This blend will ensure your gown maintains timeless allure with a modern twist.

BRIDAL BLISS

Expressing Your Passions

Your wedding day is an opportunity to celebrate not only your love for your partner but also your passions and interests. Incorporate elements of your hobbies, interests, or cultural heritage into your gown to create a look that is uniquely yours.

Whether you're a nature lover who adores floral motifs, a vintage enthusiast inspired by the glamour of bygone eras, or a traveler at heart longing to incorporate elements from different cultures, let your passions shine through in every detail of your gown.

Inspiration and Research

Gathering inspiration is a crucial part of the process. Create a mood board with images of dresses, fabrics, and details that resonate with you. Look at bridal magazines, Pinterest boards, and designer collections. Pay attention to the silhouettes, textures, and embellishments that catch your eye. This visual compilation will serve as a guide when you begin shopping for or designing your dress.

However, don't limit yourself to traditional bridal sources for inspiration. Explore fashion runways, art galleries, nature, and even architecture for unique gown features. Notice how different elements make you feel and how they align with your vision of beauty and self-expression. This broader perspective can lead to unexpected and delightful discoveries.

In conclusion, your wedding dress will be a focal point of your big day, etched into memories and photographs for years to come. Make it count by ensuring it mirrors your essence and story. A gown that encapsulates who you are and the love you share will not only make you shine on your wedding day but also serve as a cherished keepsake of this pivotal moment in your life.

Your dress is more than just a garment; it's a symbol of your love story and a reflection of your unique personality. Embrace the opportunity to express yourself through your bridal attire, from the silhouette and fabric to the smallest embellishments and details.

Whether you choose a classic gown with subtle personal touches or opt for a completely bespoke design, your goal should be to create a look that feels authentic, beautiful, and unmistakably you.

Dive into our virtual bridal-style vision board activity! Curate a collection of dress styles, fabrics, and accessories that reflect your unique personality and wedding vision.

Using digital collage tools like Canva or Pinterest, follow our simple steps to bring your wedding dress dreams to life.

Activity: Virtual Bridal Style Vision Board

Aim: To help you visualize and articulate your personal style preferences for your wedding gown independently.

Materials Needed:

Access to the internet

A computer or smartphone

A digital collage tool (such as Canva, PicMonkey, Adobe Spark or Pinterest)

Instructions:

BRIDAL BLISS

Reflection: Take some time to reflect on your personal style preferences, inspirations, and any specific ideas you have for your wedding attire. Consider the questions mentioned earlier in the brainstorming session.

Gather Inspiration: Use the internet to search for bridal fashion images, textures, colors, and any other elements that resonate with your vision for your wedding gown. Explore bridal websites, Pinterest boards, fashion blogs, and social media platforms for inspiration. Save or bookmark the images that speak to you.

Create Your Vision Board: Choose a digital collage tool or platform to create your virtual bridal-style vision board. Options include:

Canva: Sign up for a free account on Canva and use their drag-and-drop interface to create a custom collage. They offer various templates and design elements to choose from.

PicMonkey: This software offers a user-friendly interface for creating collages. You can upload your own images or choose from their library of stock photos and graphics to design your vision board.

Adobe Spark: If you prefer Adobe products, Adobe Spark allows you to create stunning visual content, including collages, with ease. Explore their templates and design features to bring your vision to life.

Pinterest: If you're using Pinterest for inspiration, create a dedicated board for your bridal style vision board. Pin images that resonate with your personal style and wedding gown preferences. You can arrange them into a cohesive visual representation of your vision by dragging and dropping pins within your board.

Review and Refine: Take a step back and review your vision board. Does it accurately capture your personal style and wedding gown preferences? Make any necessary adjustments or additions to ensure that your vision board truly reflects your unique aesthetic.

Reflection: Reflect on what you've created and how it aligns with your vision for your wedding attire. Consider how you can use your virtual bridal style vision board as a reference point during the gown selection process.

This vision board serves as a helpful reference throughout the gown selection process, ensuring that your final choice aligns with your desired aesthetic.

As we shift from celebrating individual bridal styles, we now turn to perfecting the fit with meticulous alterations and fittings, ensuring every bride looks stunning and feels comfortable.

Chapter Ten

Perfecting the Fit

Starting the quest for your dream wedding dress is a magical experience, yet ensuring it fits perfectly is just as important. The process of fittings and alterations stands as a crucial step in tailoring the gown to your unique shape, ensuring both beauty and comfort on your special day.

From the initial selection of your gown to the final fitting before you walk down the aisle, a series of adjustments are necessary to achieve that impeccable fit. These alterations are not mere formalities; they are the key to elevating your bridal look from beautiful to breathtaking.

In this chapter, we delve into the significance of these alterations, shedding light on how they enhance both the appearance and comfort of your dress. We'll guide you through the typical schedule for fittings and offer invaluable tips to ensure the best fit for your body. Whether it's a minor tweak or a major adjustment, understanding the art of bridal fittings will empower you to radiate confidence and elegance on your wedding day.

As you prepare to celebrate one of life's most cherished moments, remember that the journey towards perfection has only just begun. Embrace the significance of bridal fittings and alterations; they are the threads that weave together the fabric of your dream bridal look, ensuring that you shine with unmatched radiance as you say, "I do."

Why Bridal Fittings and Alterations Matter

Personalization: Your body is as unique as your love story, and your attire should reflect this individuality. Fittings and alterations allow garments to be tailored to your preferences. For instance, if you have a scar or prefer more coverage, adding sleeves can give you confidence. And if you want to jazz up a plain hemline, adding lace trims adds a romantic touch.

Enhanced Comfort: Comfort is key to confidence on your big day. Ill-fitting attire can spoil the fun. But through bridal fittings and precise alterations, your dress becomes both stylish and comfy. Imagine tripping over a too-long hemline or struggling with sleeves that are too long. By adjusting these, you can move freely and gracefully, ensuring a hassle-free wedding day.

Visual Cohesion: Your wedding or special event attire should be a seamless extension of your personality and style. Fittings and alterations provide the opportunity to refine every detail, ensuring visual harmony from neckline to hemline.

Attention to Detail: Attention to Detail: The beauty of your wedding dress lies in its exquisite craftsmanship and attention to detail. Every stitch, bead, and lace applique is meticulously placed to enhance the overall design and create a harmonious look.

Fittings and alterations play a crucial role in enhancing these details by ensuring the dress fits you perfectly and highlighting its intricate craftsmanship. Through precise tailoring, the dress contours to your body, accentuating your silhouette and allowing every detail to shine.

Having explored the importance of fitting and alteration for perfecting your wedding dress, let's now transition to understanding what to expect during your bridal consultation and fitting appointments.

Bridal Consultation and Fitting Expectations

Bridal fittings at the boutique typically involve several stages, beginning with the selection of the dress and culminating in the final fitting. Here's what to expect:

Initial Consultation: At the boutique, you begin your consultation by discussing your preferences, style, and budget with a bridal consultant. Based on this information, the consultant will help you select dresses to try on.

Trying on Dresses: You will try on various dresses to find the one that best suits your style and body shape. During this stage, the consultant offers guidance and suggestions to help you make an informed decision.

Measurements and Ordering: Once you've chosen your dress, the consultant will take precise measurements for the perfect fit. At your first fitting, we'll check the dress's fit and talk about any alterations needed.

Alterations: If alterations are needed, the dress is taken to an in-house seamstress or referred to a trusted external seamstress.

Common alterations include hemming, taking in or letting out the bodice, adjusting straps, and adding bustles for the train.

Additional Fittings: Depending on the complexity of the alterations, multiple fittings may be required to ensure the perfect fit. Each fitting allows the seamstress to make adjustments based on your feedback and body changes.

Final Fitting: The final fitting is scheduled closer to the wedding date to ensure that the dress fits perfectly. This fitting gives the bride the opportunity to see the completed alterations and make any final adjustments if necessary.

Pickup and Care Instructions: Once the alterations are complete, you will receive a call or email to come and collect your dress.

After understanding what to expect from your bridal fittings, let's now look into some practical tips to ensure your alteration process goes smoothly and successfully.

Tips for Alterations with Ease

Start Early: Time is crucial for the perfect fit. Start alterations early to allow for multiple fittings and adjustments. This ensures ample time for necessary changes and reduces last-minute stress, letting you enjoy the lead-up to your special day with peace of mind.

Choose a Skilled Tailor: If the boutique does not offer alterations, select a skilled and experienced tailor. Look for professionals who specialize in bridal or formal wear and have a proven track record. A skilled tailor will have the technical expertise for precise adjustments and offer valuable insights to enhance the fit and overall look of your attire.

Communicate Clearly: Effective communication is essential for conveying your vision to the tailor. Be specific about your preferences and concerns during fittings, and provide feedback throughout the process. This ensures the tailor understands your expectations and can make the necessary adjustments, resulting in an ensemble that exceeds your expectations.

Consider Undergarments: The right undergarments are essential for a perfect fit. Wear the appropriate undergarments during fittings to simulate the silhouette you'll have on the big day, whether it's a supportive bra, shapewear, or petticoat. By wearing the right undergarments, you'll ensure that the tailor can make precise adjustments that accommodate your chosen underpinnings seamlessly, resulting in a flawless fit that enhances your overall silhouette.

Plan for Movement: Your special day will be filled with moments of joy, laughter, and celebration, and your attire should allow you to move with ease and grace throughout the festivities. During fittings, take the time to move around and test the range of motion to ensure that your attire remains comfortable and unrestricted.

Final Fitting: The final fitting is your opportunity to ensure that every detail is perfect before the big day. Use this time to try on the altered garment one last time, paying close attention to the fit and overall comfort. If any final tweaks are needed, communicate them clearly to the tailor to ensure that everything is perfected to your satisfaction.

Concluding our discussion on bridal fittings and alterations, it's crucial to prioritize the perfect fit for your wedding dress. These adjustments aren't just about aesthetics; they're about ensuring you feel comfortable and confident on your special day. Remember to start the process early, collaborate closely with your tailor, and express your preferences clearly.

Now, let's transition from the excitement of fittings to the practicality of budgeting, ensuring every element of your wedding reflects both elegance and financial sensibility.

Chapter Eleven

Budgeting Brilliance

As we delve into Chapter 10 of our bridal journey, it's time to shine a spotlight on a pivotal aspect often overlooked amidst the excitement of wedding preparations: budgeting for your dream dress.

In this chapter, we explore the critical importance of budgeting for your wedding dress. Setting a budget isn't just about financial constraints; it's a strategic tool that empowers every bride to make informed decisions and ensures a harmonious balance between desires and financial realities.

Let's uncover the significance of setting a budget for your wedding dress and why it's a fundamental step for every bride on her journey to bridal bliss.

Define your Overall Wedding Dress Budget

When it comes to budgeting for your dream wedding dress, clarity and strategy are key. Before diving into the world of bridal boutiques and designer labels, take a moment to define your overall wedding dress budget. By establishing a clear budget from the outset, you can ensure that your financial goals align with your bridal vision.

Prioritization is essential to effectively allocating your funds when planning for your wedding dress. Every bride has different preferences: some prioritize renowned designers or exclusive boutiques, while others emphasize style and budget. If the designer label holds significance for you, it may be necessary to allocate a larger portion of your budget accordingly, considering that designer gowns often come with higher price tags.

By aligning your dress expenses with your personal priorities, you can create a budget that reflects your unique style and ensures financial responsibility. This approach enables you to stay within your means while still achieving the wedding dress of your dreams.

Now that we've laid the groundwork for budgeting your dream dress, let's move on to considering all the expenses involved.

Consider all Expenses

When budgeting for your dream wedding dress, it's essential to consider all associated expenses beyond just the gown itself.

BRIDAL BLISS

While the cost of the dress may be the most significant portion of your budget, there are several other expenses to keep in mind.

Start by researching average costs for alterations in your area and factoring these into your dress budget. Be sure to include allowances for multiple fittings and alterations. Additionally, inquire about any additional charges upfront when shopping for your dress to avoid any surprises later on.

Accessories such as shoes, veil, jewelry, and undergarments play a crucial role in elevating your look and completing your bridal ensemble. These items can add up quickly, so it's important to allocate a portion of your budget specifically for accessories.

By considering all expenses associated with your dress upfront, you can create a more accurate and comprehensive budget that ensures you're financially prepared for every aspect of your bridal look.

Having covered the various expenses to anticipate, let's now look into researching average costs for your dream dress.

Research Average Costs

Before you start shopping for your wedding dress, it's crucial to know the average cost of wedding dresses. Research thoroughly to understand the price ranges in your area or preferred market. Prices vary due to factors like designer, fabric quality, and embellishments.

Explore bridal boutiques, online stores, and designer collections to see the range of prices and styles. Take note of features like lace detailing and beadwork that affect pricing. Compare prices across different sources to ensure you're getting the best value.

Once you have a clear picture, refine your budget accordingly. Stay flexible throughout the process and be willing to adjust your budget as needed.

With a clear understanding of researching average costs, let's now explore the importance of being realistic about your budget and expectations.

Be Realistic

When it comes to budgeting for your wedding dress, it's crucial to be realistic about what you can afford and what aligns with your overall financial goals. Start by assessing your current financial situation and determining how much you're comfortable spending on your dress.

In addition to considering your current financial circumstances, be realistic about your expectations and priorities when it comes to your wedding dress. While it's natural to want the perfect gown that makes you feel like a princess, it's essential to balance your desires with practical considerations.

Now that we've discussed being realistic about budget and expectations, let's explore opportunities to maximize your budget through package deals and second-hand options.

Leveraging Sales and Promotions

Many bridal boutiques and designers offer package deals or discounts for purchasing multiple items, such as the dress, veil, shoes, and accessories, together. Take advantage of these opportunities to maximize your budget and get the most value for your money.

Research bridal shops and designers in your area to identify those that offer package deals or discounts. Be prepared to negotiate and advocate for yourself to secure the best possible deal. Many bridal boutiques are open to negotiation, especially if you're willing to pay cash or make a larger upfront payment.

In addition, exploring second-hand or sample sales is a smart move for budget-conscious brides seeking their dream dress without the hefty price tag. Second-hand dresses, often significantly discounted, offer the chance to snag a designer gown at a fraction of the retail cost. Additionally, sample sales by boutiques or designers provide access to high-quality dresses at reduced prices.

When considering second-hand or sample sales, inspect dresses thoroughly for any damage or wear. With careful consideration, you can find a stunning wedding dress at a fraction of the cost, achieving your bridal vision without breaking the bank.

Having explored cost-saving options, let's now consider the importance of allocating a contingency fund for unexpected expenses.

Set Aside a Contingency Fund

Allocating a contingency fund for your wedding attire is both a prudent financial move and a practical necessity that can mitigate stress and streamline your planning process. A contingency fund affords you peace of mind and flexibility in decision-making. By having the resources to address unforeseen expenses, such as alterations costing more than anticipated, rush fees for last-minute changes, or expedited delivery, you can make informed choices without feeling constrained by financial limitations.

To determine the appropriate size of your contingency fund, consider allocating a percentage of your overall dress budget rather than a fixed amount. This ensures your contingency fund scales proportionally with your dress expenses, providing sufficient coverage for any surprises that may arise.

With a contingency fund in place, let's now emphasize the importance of avoiding impulse purchases to stay within your budget.

Avoid Impulse Purchases

One of the most important aspects of budgeting for your wedding dress is to resist the temptation of impulse purchases. While it's easy to get swept up in the excitement of wedding dress shopping and fall in love with the first gown you try on, making an impulse purchase can lead to overspending and buyer's remorse.

Instead, take your time to carefully consider your options and make an informed decision that aligns with your budget and overall vision for your wedding day. If you find yourself tempted to make an impulse purchase, take a step back and give yourself time to think it over.

In conclusion, budgeting for your dream wedding dress requires careful planning and prioritization. By defining your budget, considering all expenses, and exploring cost-saving options like negotiating package deals or shopping second-hand, you can find your perfect dress without overspending.

Remember to allocate funds for alterations and accessories and set aside a contingency fund for unexpected expenses. With strategic budgeting, you can achieve your bridal vision while staying within your financial means.

Transitioning from the concept of setting a budget for the wedding dress, let's now introduce the Wedding Dress Shopping

BRIDAL BLISS

Budget Worksheet, designed to assist brides in establishing a clear and manageable budget specifically tailored to their dress.

Wedding Dress Shopping Budget Worksheet

Total Budget for Wedding Dress: _____

Estimated Cost Breakdown:

Wedding Dress:

Base Cost: $_____

Taxes: $_____

Shipping Fees: $_____

Total: $_____

Alterations:

Hemming: $_____

Taking In/Out: $_____

Bustle: $_____

Other (Specify): $_____

Total: $_____

Accessories:

Veil: $_____

Shoes: $_____

Jewelry (necklace, earrings, bracelet): $_____

Hair Accessories: $_____

Other: $_____

Total: $_____

Undergarments:

Bridal Bra: $_____

Shapewear: $_____

Petticoat/Crinoline: $_____

Other (Specify): $_____

BRIDAL BLISS

Total: $_____

Miscellaneous:

Dry Cleaning: $_____

Preservation: $_____

Garment Bag: $_____

Insurance: $_____

Contingency Fund: $_____

Other (Specify): $_____

Total: $_____

Total Estimated Expenses: _____

Additional Expense: _____

Instructions:

Enter your total budget for the wedding dress.

Estimate costs for: dress, alterations, accessories, undergarments etc.

Calculate the total estimated expenses.

Calculate the remaining budget. Use the "Notes" section for additional expenses or comments.

Chapter Twelve

Shopping Etiquette for Bridal Gowns

Shopping etiquette is essential for a smooth and pleasant experience, benefiting both the bride and the bridal boutique staff. Following these guidelines allows brides to manage the dress shopping journey with grace, respecting and appreciating the expertise and assistance provided by bridal consultants.

This chapter offers valuable insights into the etiquette to observe when seeking the ideal bridal gown. By understanding and implementing these etiquette guidelines, brides can make the most of their time with bridal consultants, minimize potential misunderstandings, and ultimately find the dress that fulfills their bridal dreams.

Let's explore the following bridal etiquette stated in this chapter:

Schedule Appointments

Scheduling appointments ensures brides receive personalized attention from consultants, respects the time and resources of boutique staff, avoids overcrowding, maximizes efficiency, and enhances the overall shopping experience by creating a relaxed and memorable environment.

Be Punctual

Being punctual shows respect for the time and schedules of the bridal boutique staff and other customers. It ensures that brides can fully utilize their allotted appointment time, helps maintain the boutique's schedule, and allows for a smoother, more efficient shopping experience. Punctuality also demonstrates consideration and professionalism, setting a positive tone for the entire dress shopping process.

Communicate Preferences

Effective communication with your bridal consultant is key to finding the perfect dress. Clearly articulate your style preferences, including details such as silhouette, fabric, neckline, and embellishments. Providing this information upfront helps the consultant narrow down the options and tailor their recommendations to suit your taste and budget.

Stay Open-Minded

While you may have a particular style or silhouette in mind when shopping for your wedding dress, it's essential to remain open-minded. This will allow you to consider a variety of styles and suggestions from consultants, potentially discovering unexpected favorites. This flexibility enhances the shopping experience and increases the chances of finding the perfect gown.

Respect Boutique Policies

Familiarize yourself with the policies of each bridal boutique regarding photography, returns, and alterations. Some boutiques may restrict photography to protect their designs, while others may have specific return policies and alteration processes. Respecting these guidelines ensures a hassle-free shopping experience and prevents misunderstandings.

Provide Honest Feedback

Your bridal consultant depends on your feedback to grasp your preferences and steer you toward the ideal dress. Be honest and transparent about your impressions of each dress you try on. If there are elements you dislike or feel uneasy about, tactfully communicate them to the consultant. Conversely, if you adore a dress, articulate what aspects resonate with you. Constructive feedback enables the consultant to fine-tune their recommendations, leading to a dress that embodies your vision.

Limit Dresses in the Fitting Room

Limiting dresses in the fitting room demonstrates consideration and respect for both the boutique staff and other brides. By restricting the number of dresses, you help maintain an organized and efficient environment, allowing staff to assist you and other customers effectively. It also shows appreciation for the boutique's resources and time.

Wear Proper Undergarments

While personal preferences vary, it's advisable to select undergarments that prioritize both modesty and comfort during bridal fittings. Avoid overly revealing styles such as thongs or excessively sheer fabrics, as they may detract from the focus on finding the perfect wedding gown. Opt instead for seamless styles that offer adequate coverage while maintaining a sense of modesty. This ensures a professional and respectful atmosphere during fittings, allowing the focus to remain on achieving the bride's desired look and fit for her special day.

Mind Your Budget

Being mindful of your budget shows respect for your financial resources and those of the bridal boutique. By setting clear budget parameters, you streamline the dress selection process, allowing the consultant to present options within your price range. Openly discussing your budget with the consultant also prevents any awkward situations during the appointment and enables the consultant to offer valuable guidance tailored to your financial limitations.

Inquire about Alterations

Discussing alterations upfront fosters clarity and prevents misunderstandings, aligning both you and the boutique staff on the necessary modifications.

Take Your Time

Shopping for a wedding dress is a significant decision, and it's essential not to rush the process. Take your time to consider each dress carefully, envisioning yourself wearing it on your special day. Allow yourself the opportunity to explore different options, try on multiple styles, and revisit dresses you're unsure about before making a final decision.

Celebrate the Moment

Finding your dream wedding dress is a milestone worth celebrating, so be sure to acknowledge the significance of the moment. Take a moment to pause and reflect on the excitement and joy of discovering the dress that makes you feel beautiful and confident. Share the experience with your entourage and celebrate together, whether it's with a toast, a round of applause, or simply a heartfelt expression of gratitude.

Express Gratitude

Show appreciation to the bridal consultant and boutique staff for their assistance and expertise throughout your shopping experience. Even if you don't find the perfect dress during your visit, express gratitude for their time and attention.

Finalize the Purchase

Finalizing the purchase of your wedding dress symbolizes respect for the process and commitment to your choice. This also honors the efforts of both you and the bridal boutique staff in finding the perfect gown. By completing the transaction, you secure your dream dress for your special day, affirming your confidence in the decision-making process.

In summary, observing proper etiquette when shopping for a bridal gown ensures a positive and memorable experience for both you and the boutique staff. By following these etiquette guidelines, you can navigate the dress shopping process with confidence, respect, and grace, ultimately finding the dress of your dreams and creating lasting memories along the way.

Alicia Hernandez-Whyle

ABOUT AUTHOR

Alicia Hernandez-Whyle is not just a bridal boutique owner; she is a seasoned expert with over a decade of dedicated service to brides worldwide. Her journey in the bridal industry began as a heartfelt mission to assist brides in navigating the intricate process of selecting the attire that embodies their dreams for their special day. With each bride she encounters, Alicia brings a wealth of expertise and insight, honed over years of working closely with individuals to create unforgettable wedding experiences.

Driven by her passion for excellence and unwavering commitment to customer satisfaction, Alicia has earned a sterling reputation as a trusted advisor and confidante to countless brides. Her boutique isn't just a place to find a dress; it's a sanctuary where brides can find support, guidance, and the reassurance they need as they embark on one of life's most significant journeys.

Alicia's dedication to her craft goes beyond mere transactions; it's about creating magical moments and fostering lasting memories. Her approach to bridal fashion is both personalized and profound, as she understands that each bride is unique and their journey to finding the perfect dress is as individual as they are.

BRIDAL BLISS

In her role as an author, Alicia is honored to share her wealth of knowledge and passion for bridal fashion with readers. Through her contributions to Bridal Bliss: A Guide to Choosing Your Perfect Wedding Dress, she seeks to inspire and empower brides as they navigate the exciting path to wedded bliss. With Alicia's guidance, brides can embark on their wedding dress journey with confidence, knowing they have a seasoned expert by their side every step of the way.

www.ingramcontent.com/pod-product-compliance
Lightning Source LLC
LaVergne TN
LVHW021333080526
838202LV00003B/154